The story of feather dusters

MADE IN SOUTH AFRICA

Lynn Barnes

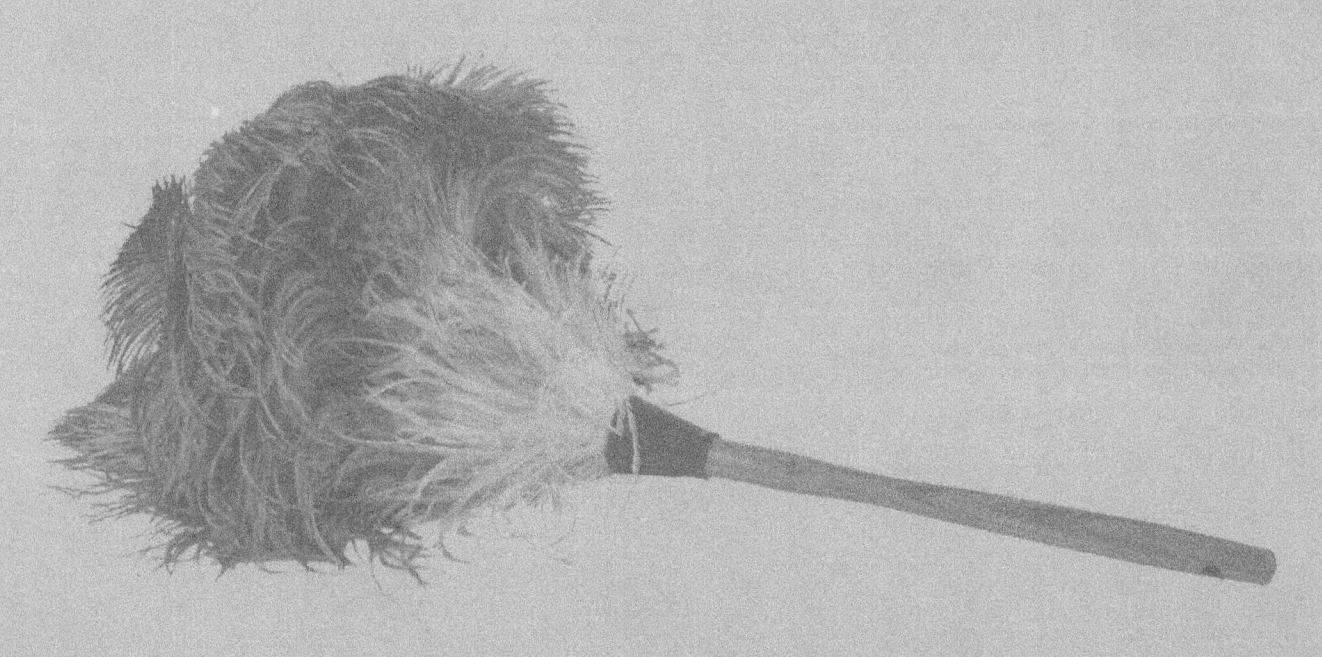

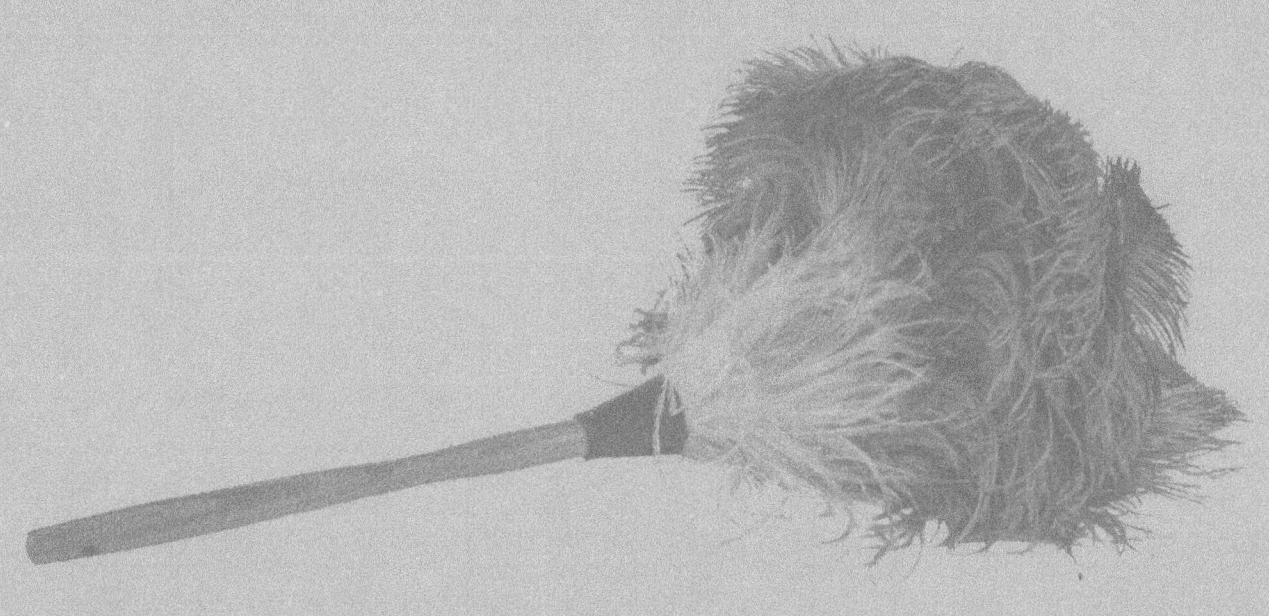

Words that are in bold, like **this**, are explained in the Word help, on the page and at the end of the book.

The *Made in South Africa* series is published by
Awareness Publishing Group (Pty) Ltd.
Copyright © 2019

Awareness Publishing (SA) (Pty) Ltd
www.awareness.co.za
info@awareness.co.za
+27 (0)86 110 1491
www.facebook.com/AwarenessPublishing

All rights reserved. No part of this publication may be reproduced in any form without written permission from the publisher, except by a reviewer.

First edition 2019

The story of feather dusters by Lynn Barnes
ISBN 978-1-77008-995-2

Summary: A simple introduction to feather dusters and how they are made from ostrich feathers.

Book design: Richard Keenan-Smith and Elizabeth Barnard

Editorial credits: Managing editor: Monique le Riché; Copy editor: Danya Ristić-Schacherl; Picture editors: Anne Laing and Lawrence Frank

Picture credits: Cover © Jeremy Glyn; cover (background) © kubikactive; cover (flag) © Kurt / Dreamstime; endpapers © rodeen / Fotolia; p4 © AAI Fotostock SA / Alamy / Arco Images GmbH; p6 © artush / Fotolia; p8 © AAI Fotostock SA / Michael Krabs; p8 (inset) © evbrbe / Fotolia; p10 (top) © Christine / Fotolia; p10 (bottom) © zea_lenanet / Fotolia; p12 © Brown Reference Group / Elizabeth Barnard & Bianca Keenan-Smith; p14 © Jan van der Poll; p16 © AAI Fotostock SA / Alamy / Photononstop; p18 © AAI Fotostock SA / Alamy / Arco Images GmbH; p20 © Gallo Images / Juhan Kuus; p21 © Jan van der Poll; p22 (top) © AAI Fotostock SA / Alamy / Dinodia Photos; p22 (bottom) © Jan van der Poll; p24 (all) © Jan van der Poll; p26 © AAI Fotostock SA / Dinodia Photo; p28 © Jeremy Glyn; p30 © Jeremy Glyn; p32 © Gallo Images / Getty Images / Jeff J Mitchell; p34 © Jan van der Poll

The author would like to thank Vanessa Engelbrecht of Safari Ostrich Farm and Peter Liebenberg of Klein Karoo International Feathers for reviewing the manuscript and providing additional information.

1 3 5 7 9 0 8 6 4 2

Contents

A useful tool for cleaning 5
Ostriches 7
A bird that cannot fly 9
Different feathers 11
Ostrich farming 13
More than just feathers 15
Ostrich eggs 17
Ostrich feathers 19
Collecting the feathers 21
At the factory 23
Putting the parts together 25
Brightly coloured dusters 27
Special handles 29
Packaging 31
South Africa sells ostrich feather dusters to the world 33
Word help 35

Feather dusters for sale by the side of the road.

A useful tool for cleaning

A feather duster is very useful for cleaning things in and around the home. It is a tool made from the feathers of a bird called an ostrich. In many places, feather dusters are sold at the side of the road. They come in different sizes and colours.

A male ostrich (on the left) and a female (on the right), with their babies.

Ostriches

Ostriches are the largest birds in the world. An adult ostrich can be taller than a man and can weigh as much as two men. An ostrich has a small head; a long, thin neck; a large body and long, thin legs.

Adult male ostriches have black and white feathers. Females and young males have greyish-brown feathers. There are no feathers on the neck or legs of male or female ostriches.

Did you know?

Ostriches do not have any teeth. They swallow small stones to help grind up the food that they eat.

Ostriches can run at more than 70 kilometres an hour.
Inset: Ostriches have two toes on each foot.

A bird that cannot fly

Ostriches have very small wings, which are not strong enough to lift their big, heavy bodies up into the air. So ostriches are not able to fly.

But they can run very fast. Most other birds have three or four toes on their feet. Ostriches have only two toes, which helps them to run faster. Their long legs allow them to cover up to 5 metres with one **stride**.

> **Word help**
> **stride:** a long step made while running

A bird's feather held together with its tiny hooks is smooth and stiff.

An ostrich feather is soft and fluffy.

Different feathers

The feathers of most birds have tiny hooks on them that hold the parts of the feather together. This keeps the feathers stiff and helps the birds to fly.

Ostrich feathers do not have these little hooks. The feathers are soft and can bend in all directions. So they make good feather dusters. The feathers pick up dust well and can get into small places.

The area around Oudtshoorn in Western Cape is an important ostrich farming area. The feathers from its many ostrich farms are sold all over the world.

Ostrich farming

Farmers started to keep ostriches in the Klein Karoo area of South Africa in 1864. This was a difficult time for farmers in that area because there had been no rain for a long time and all their **crops** were dying.

> **Word help**
> **crops:** plants grown for food

But ostriches are very strong birds. They can live in hot, dry places and do not need to drink water. They get all the water they need from the plants that they eat.

Beautifully painted ostrich eggshells.

More than just feathers

There are now about 450 ostrich farms in South Africa, mainly in Western Cape. At first, farmers kept ostriches mainly for their feathers, but nowadays ostriches provide other things too:

- Ostrich meat has become very popular because it tastes like beef. But it is healthier because it has very little fat.
- Ostrich eggshells are painted or decorated with patterns. Many people like to buy these eggshells to put in their homes.
- Ostrich skin is made into leather for purses and bags.

A man putting an ostrich egg into an incubator.

Ostrich eggs

Ostriches lay eggs during the warmer months from August to May. The eggs are very large and have strong, thick shells.

In the wild, ostriches build a nest on the ground. They sit on the eggs to protect them and keep them warm until the baby ostriches break out of their shells, or hatch.

On farms, the farmer collects the eggs and puts them in a special warm cupboard called an incubator. After about 42 days, the eggs hatch.

Did you know?
An ostrich egg is more than 20 times bigger than a chicken's egg. It can weigh more than 2 kilograms!

The feathers on the body are shorter than the feathers on the wings.

Ostrich feathers

Ostriches have several layers of feathers that protect their bodies and keep them warm. The feathers are different sizes, from short to very long.

The birds can live for more than 40 years and grow new feathers all the time. Older feathers start to get loose, ready to fall out and make way for new feathers.

Ostriches on a farm.

Collecting the feathers

About every six months the farmers carefully take out or cut off some of the older feathers from the wings and tails of the ostriches. This does not hurt the birds, and new feathers soon grow. The farmers sell the feathers they collect to be made into feather dusters.

Farm workers cutting feathers from an ostrich.

A worker washing the feathers.

Factory workers sorting the feathers.

At the factory

Before the feathers can be used to make dusters, they go to a factory. Here the feathers are washed to remove any dirt. Then they are sprayed with special liquids to kill any **germs** and insects.

The clean feathers are sorted according to size and how good they are. When the feathers are ready, they are sent to an **assembly plant**.

> **Word help**
>
> **germs:** very tiny living things that can cause illness
>
> **assembly plant:** a factory where different parts are collected and put together to make something

Cutting the feathers to the same length.

Attaching the feathers to the handle.

Attaching the plastic cap.

A finished duster.

Putting the parts together

Workers make feather dusters by attaching a group of feathers to a handle. First the bottom parts of the feathers are stuck to the handle with glue. Then wire is wrapped around the glued part to hold it firm. Finally, a plastic cap is pushed over the wire. This makes the duster look neat, and stops the wire from hurting anyone.

Workers dyeing feathers a bright pink colour.

Brightly coloured dusters

The natural colour of ostrich feathers is black, white or greyish-brown. But the colour of the feathers can be changed by soaking them in special coloured liquids called **dyes**. Feather dusters are made in all sorts of bright colours. The feathers are coloured first and then attached to the handle in the usual way.

> **Word help**
>
> **dyes:** coloured liquids used to change the colour of something

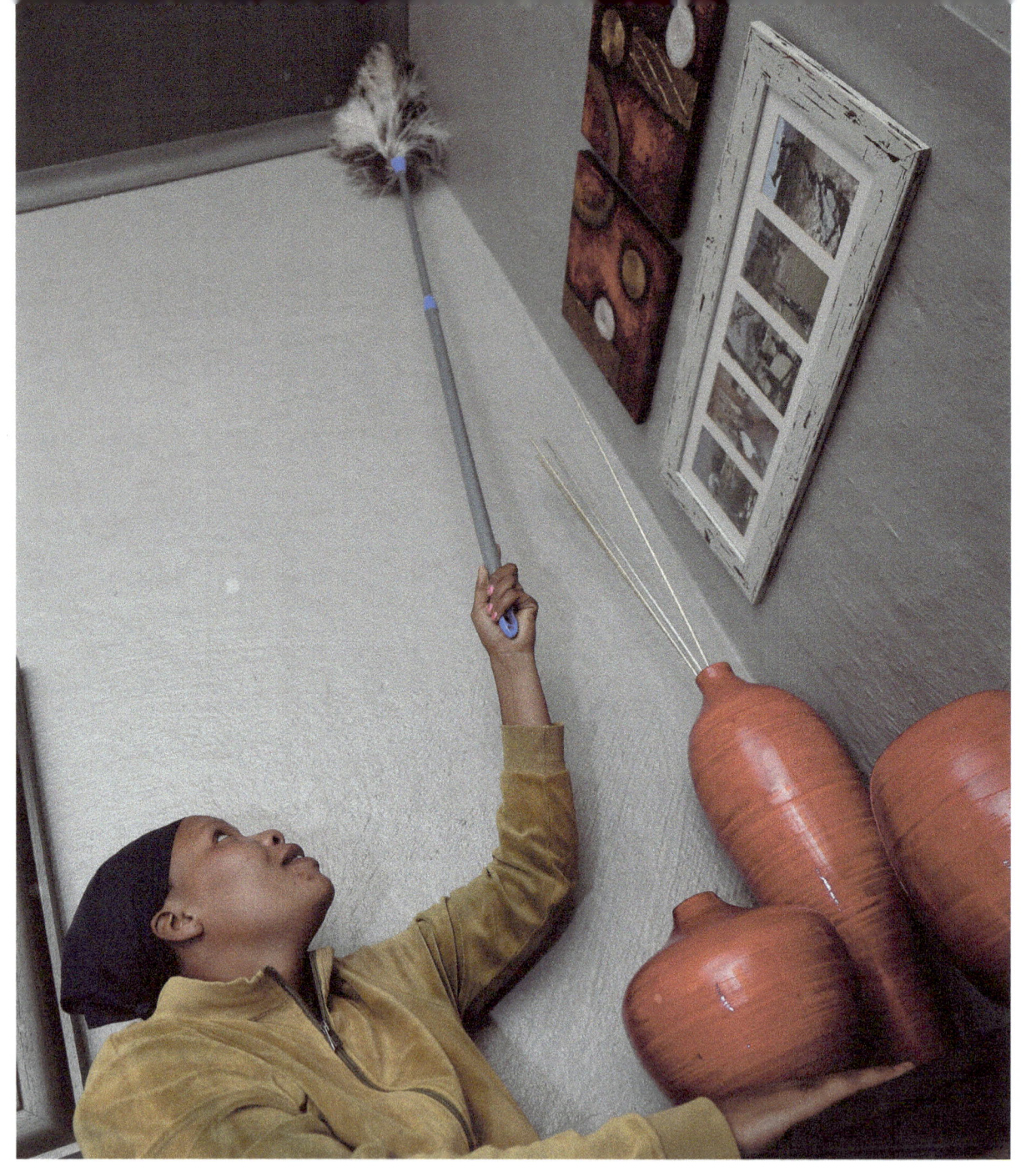

A feather duster with a long handle is good for dusting high places.

Special handles

Most feather dusters have a group of feathers attached to a short wooden or plastic handle. But some dusters have a special handle with two parts – one inside the other. The inside part can slide out to make the handle longer. This makes the duster useful for reaching high places.

A feather duster in its packaging.

Packaging

Once the dusters are finished, they are packed in plastic covers. The covers are tight enough to keep the feathers in place, but not tight enough to break them. The cover is also a bit longer than the feathers so that the ends do not get bent or broken. Then the finished dusters are sent to be sold.

A woman dusting pictures with a feather duster in an art gallery in Scotland, United Kingdom.

South Africa sells ostrich feather dusters to the world

South Africa is one of the only places in the world where there are ostrich farms that produce feathers specially for making feather dusters. More than 2 billion feather dusters are made in South Africa every year and sold to countries all over the world.

> **Did you know?**
> 2 billion is two thousand million or 2 000 000 000. That is a lot of feather dusters!

A worker sorting dyed feathers according to size.

Word help

assembly plant: a factory where different parts are collected and put together to make something

crops: plants grown for food

dyes: coloured liquids used to change the colour of something

germs: very tiny living things that can cause illness

stride: a long step made while running